SCRIPTURE SCRIBBLES

SCRIPTURE SCRIBBLES: CARTOONS FROM THE CHOIR LOFT

PHILLIP DILLMAN

Published 2014 by HumorOutcasts Press
Printed in the United States of America

ISBN 0-692-31602-7
EAN-13 978-069231602-3

ACKNOWLEDGMENTS

Jesus - for being a good sport.

Foreword

"Now there are varieties of gifts, but the same Spirit."

So writes the Apostle Paul in his first letter to the church in Corinth. To this I would add, "There are varieties of responses to God's word proclaimed, but the same Spirit."

It has been my privilege to serve as Phil Dillman's pastor for more than thirteen years. Early in my time at the church, I would receive an occasional "Scribble" from Phil after worship—a cartoon that incorporated the theme of the service. Many times, his work had to do with the scripture and sermon, but other times it had to do with a hymn verse or line of a prayer. Often these sketches that revealed Phil's dry sense of humor and out-of-the-box reflection made me laugh out loud.

Phil's interpretation can be subtle or obvious, and I marvel at how he connects his art to the gospel message. Phil has said that drawing during the service helps him listen more attentively. Who knew that "Scribbles" could be such a powerful spiritual practice?

Over the years, Phil's creative response to God's word in worship has become a weekly discipline, and the congregation looks forward to seeing his latest creation at Heavenly Perks fellowship time. Even guest preachers look for Phil after the service. We are delighted that Phil has taken time to compile a collection of "Scribbles" for others to experience. I hope readers will take the time to reflect on the gospel message contained in his offerings.

With thanksgiving to God for the creative movement of the Holy Spirit in Phil,

Rev. Dr. Nancy Jo Dederer, Pastor
First Presbyterian Church of Homewood

Introduction

I have always been a fan of cartoons. At the age of 11, my family and I took a vacation to Washington, D.C. and, instead of spending my souvenir money on any of the typical tourist items, I opted for a Dennis the Menace cartoon book. My parents questioned the purchase but understood that it was my money that I was spending. That pocketbook was packed with so much action and humor, which I thoroughly enjoyed, that I still have it. We always had Peanuts cartoon books at our house as well. Although the pictures are simple, the humor can be complex and deep. I have always loved the laughter that cartoons inspire, and since my youth, I have spent a lot of my time trying to capture that comedy magic with my own drawings.

I can remember sitting at restaurants with my mother, and as we waited for our food to arrive, I would ask her for suggestions on what to draw. My mother, who possessed her own brand of humor, would offer silly responses such as "draw a bath" or "draw flies" or "draw a gun" before she gave me her real suggestions. I tried to draw whatever she asked for.

My drawing has always been intuitive for me. I never took a lesson, and I never thought I was talented in the sense that I draw well. But my cartoons did make people laugh, and I enjoyed that feeling immensely.

People often ask me how I combined the cartoons with church. Well, it was a natural evolution. My sister and I always attended Sunday school, and church and faith were center in our lives. When I entered high school, my mother forced me to join the school choir. While I groaned about it initially, I did learn a little about reading and understanding music. Later on, my friends thought it would be cool to form a band, and being a typical teenage guy, I agreed. So, I bought myself a small drum set followed by a 12-string acoustic guitar and a decent keyboard, all of which I taught myself to play. I even composed and recorded my own songs, and I was able to develop my vocals. The music never reached the professional level, though, as I had too many other interests that demanded my attention plus I started my career of truck driving around that time which requires a lot of hours.

A few years ago, my wife and mother-in-law were in our church choir and they told me there was a lack of men. I reluctantly joined but found that I actually enjoyed it, and this experience has made me a stronger singer plus it gave me the inspiration I needed to draw my Scripture Scribbles.

The first cartoon I did was for our pastor. She started off a sermon stating that pretty much everything that had to do with water reminded her of her own baptism. Having the literal and twisted sense of humor that I do, I decided to draw an image of someone with a scowl on his face standing in water in a flooded basement. The cartoon character is handing a box to someone on a ladder who has been placing other boxes on a shelf out of harm's way of the flood. The person on the ladder is asking the one in the water, "Does this remind you of your baptism?" That scribble gave the pastor a good laugh, and that one cartoon sparked my desire to illustrate the sermons or scripture lessons in a humorous or abstract way.

My cartoons are truly scribbles. I draw them at church mostly during the sermons. It takes me about 15 minutes from beginning to end or conception of an idea to the final stroke of the pencil. I write the scribbles on any paper that I find. This is why in this book, some cartoons look as if they are drawn on scraps of paper or on the back of the church bulletin. In other words, these cartoons are the original drawings. I have not polished them or tried to give them a more finished look; I don't take the cartoons home and work on them and bring them back to church the next week. They are as they were drawn during our services. On truly inspirational days, I might even attempt two cartoons.

The cartoons are now expected by our church members, and they wait to see each week's drawing. On the rare occasion that I am unable to get one completed (I do have to sing in the choir!), their disappointment is visible. My goal with my cartoons is to provide people with a laugh and to make them also think about the sermon lessons in a different way. I guess the cartoons for me also force me to analyze the same old lessons that I've heard over the years. They refresh the familiar for me.

I do love the reaction that people have to my cartoons. I find it interesting how different people will simply smile at a cartoon while others will laugh out loud at the same cartoon. A few people have put forth the theory that I like to show off my drawings as a way to get attention. In truth, my drawings are a way for me to allow people the chance to smile or laugh at some of the many bible stories that have become stale over time. I think that if my drawings help me to better remember what we have just been told in the sermon, it will help others do the same. Sometimes a good laugh can help people forget about some of the trials and challenges they deal with on a day-to-day basis. I guess there are times when folks might be shocked at some of the drawings, but I hope the scribbles will be enjoyed or at least appreciated. And honestly, I hope that those who read Scripture Scribbles: Cartoons from the Choir Loft and get a chuckle or laugh from the drawings, pass the book onto others who are in need of an emotional lift in their lives as well.

I might not think I am a great artist or cartoonist, but what I do know is that God has a sense of humor, and if this is a way to get that sense of humor across to everyone, I'm good with it.

"CHOICES"

CHURCH –
ADMISSION IS FREE
BENEFIT –
ETERNAL LIFE

THEME PARK –
ADMISSION $50⁰⁰ PER PERSON
BENEFIT –
ONE DAY OF FUN
10·12·14

C'MON, PEOPLE. I ONLY GAVE YOU TEN LAWS TO FOLLOW.

10·5·14

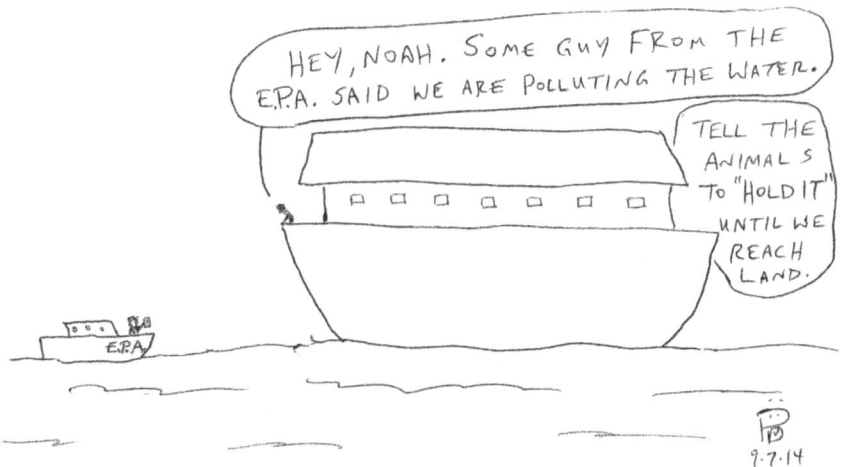

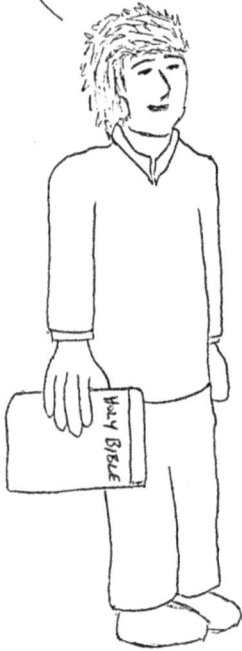

"JESUS TEACHES THE DISCIPLES"

9·23·12

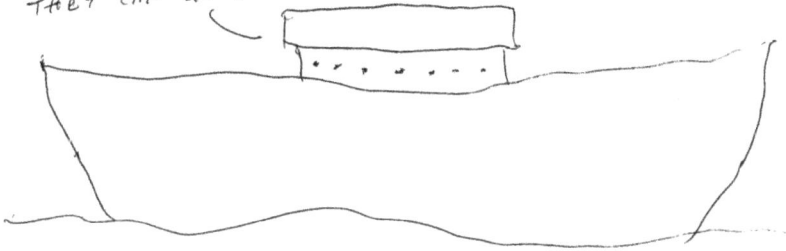

TELL EACH PAIR OF ANIMALS THAT, WHEN NATURE CALLS, THEY CAN GO TO THE "POOP" DECK.

WHAT DO YOU MEAN YOU'RE SEASICK?

THIS STEAK IS DELICIOUS, SHEM! WAIT A MINUTE... WHERE IS THE COW?

C'MON, ONE MORE TIME. 9980 TTLES OF BEER ON THE WALL, 99 BOTTLES OF BEER...

THE ULTIMATE
"POWER SUPPLY"

4·22·12

ABRAHAM AND SARAH GO FORTH, AS GOD INSTRUCTED, WITH ALL OF THEIR DESCENDANTS.

GOD'S PREFERRED CALENDAR

MISUNDERSTANDING,
SIMON AND ANDREW
CAST "ANNETTE" INTO
THE SEA.

"I JUST DON'T THINK I'M DESERVING OF THE ULTIMATE GIFT."

1-29-12

♪ I'VE GOT THE
WORLD ON A STRING.

I'M SITTIN' ON A
RAINBOW ♫

Today's Text: Psalm 23:6
*"Surely goodness and mercy shall follow me
all the days of my life;
And I shall dwell in the house of the Lord forever."*

Today's Image: Power of God
by Anneke Kai

PHIL WOULD OFTEN
GET CARRIED AWAY
WITH HIS DOODLING
IN CHURCH.
12·28·08

NOW, DOES ANYONE ELSE IN THE CONGREGATION THINK WE SHOULD ABANDON OUR CUSTOMARY FUND RAISER?

10·27·13

THE DISCIPLES PREPARE FOR THE LAST LUNCH.

"SHOUT, HOSANNAH! OH, DON'T YOU CRY FOR ME. I SING MY RESURRECTION WITH MY BANJO ON MY KNEE!"

"FISHERS OF MEN"

GABRIEL SOON LEARNED THAT SOME ANGELS NEED TO EXPLORE THEIR OTHER TALENTS.

The End

About the Author:

Phillip Dillman is a truck driver with more hobbies and interests than he has time for. He likes history of all kinds and enjoys learning and sharing his knowledge of those interests. Thus, he is Editor of the quarterly newsletter "Dillman Descendants & Ancestors" as well as the Librarian/ Archivist for the Dillman Family Association. Phillip is a fanatical collector of anything related to Pepsi-Cola, including the flavors they own such as Mountain Dew, etc. For this reason, he has also assumed the role of Editor of the quarterly newsletter of the Pepsi-Cola Collectors Club. Other history-based interests led him to become the Historian of the First

Presbyterian Church of Homewood , Illinois and to join the Homewood Rail (Heritage) Committee.

Phillip has always enjoyed drawing cartoons—not professionally, but simply to make people smile or laugh. Occasionally, he can even get a groan from a bad (or good) pun—anything to help people momentarily forget about the dukey that often creeps into their day!

www.ingramcontent.com/pod-product-compliance
Lightning Source LLC
LaVergne TN
LVHW011334080426
835513LV00006B/349